## THE LANDSCAPE OF IMAGINATION

Like its people, the landscape of North America became a place of fantasy, based on the descriptions of early travellers overawed by its sheer size and the extremes of both its scenery and climate. Early paintings by European artists were often influenced more by their own romantic notions of the New World than by any first-hand experience. To those early artists who *did* travel through the landscape of North America, it was a land of unimaginable beauty. The German-born painter Albert Bierstadt (1830-1902) travelled west with surveying expeditions and painted what he saw. His huge paintings of the Rocky Mountains and the Yosemite Valley are made even more awe-inspiring by the accuracy with which they were observed.

### AMERICA

Idealized natives became the inspiration for European writers and artists, appearing in fanciful form in paintings, illustrations and sculpture. Engravings like this one were called, like so many works of art relating to the New World, simply *America*.

### THE NOBLE SAVAGE

From their first contact, the native peoples of the Americas exerted a great fascination over European adventurers and colonists. In person, they were likened to ancient Greeks, and admired for the natural simplicity of their lives. The concept of the 'noble savage' soon became fashionable throughout Europe. Natives from the Americas were paraded like trophies before their royal patrons by triumphantly returning explorers.

# THE INDIAN NATIONS

The first people to inhabit the vast lands of North America, arrived at the end of the Ice Age – about 15,000 years ago. Crossing the narrow land bridge which then joined the north-eastern corner of Asia to the westernmost tip of Alaska, they followed game into the untouched lands revealed by the receding ice. Over the centuries, more and more people came. They spread out over the whole of the western hemisphere to the tip of South America. Another group arrived 6,000 years ago and colonized the far north – the Eskimos. The immigrants remained in small, separated groups and different ways of life evolved. They became many 'nations': some built homes in the northern woods; some, cities in stone in the desert mountains; some were river-based; while others roamed freely after the buffalo on the great open plains. Customs and cultures grew, based on a close association with the land itself and the creatures on it. By 1491 there were 15,000,000 Indians living in what is now the United States and Canada – not very many people for such a vast space. Many welcomed the newcomers, for they had legends, too – of tall fair-skinned men in flowing clothes, arriving *'out of the sea on floating islands covered with tall trees.'* Myth and reality were about to meet.

## WHY INDIANS?

When Christopher Columbus reached the islands of the Caribbean in 1492, he was convinced that he had reached his objective – India. He mistakenly called the lands he visited the 'Indies' and the native peoples 'Indians'. Five hundred years before, the Vikings encountered natives who loved red so much that they smeared their faces with red ochre from the earth. They called these brown-skinned people the 'redmen' or 'redskins'. Neither name was meant in an insulting way – rather the reverse. The names were widely used in reference to the native of both North and South America, and they became forever known as American Indians.

## THE ANASAZI

The Anasazi were the prehistoric ancestors of the pueblo Indians of the Southwest. Their civilization lasted from about 200 BC to AD 1300, during which they built the great cliff dwelling at Mesa Verde. These spears found in Utah date from that period. A very mysterious people, their name in Navajo means 'enemy ancestors'.

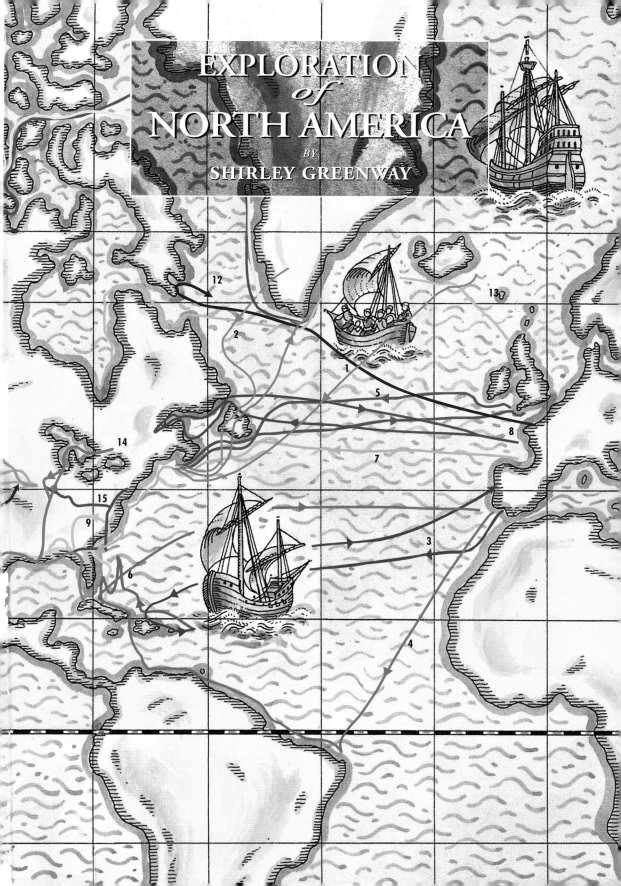

# EXPLORATION
## *of*
# NORTH AMERICA
### *BY*
### SHIRLEY GREENWAY

# THE UNKNOWN LAND

## THE NEW WORLD

Amerigo Vespucci (1454-1512) was an Italian merchant, navigator and self-publicist. He claimed to have made four voyages to the lands in the west. After the first, in 1497, Vespucci claimed to have sighted a vast new continent (South America). After further voyages with Spanish expeditions in 1501 to 1502, he wrote a famous letter calling his earlier discovery *Mundus Novus*, the 'New World' – the first person to do so.

**W**hen, in 1498, Christopher Columbus finally set foot on the South American mainland, he realized at last that he had found *'a very great continent, until today unknown.'* On his three previous voyages he had explored the islands and coastline, and it had been his unshakable belief that he had reached the fabled shores of India. However, to its first European explorers, North America was a big disappointment. It was the wrong place at the wrong time; too big, too empty and too much in the way of their real objective. It was discovered accidentally, and when discovered, it wasn't wanted. But the lure was strong – of knowledge, adventure, wealth and glory. Many came. Some searched for gold and, finding none, moved on. Some found death and never-ending fame. The French came and built a trading empire on fur and friendship. The English came, looking for new lands to colonize, and stayed to make it so. Those who saw that the New World wasn't just the route to wealth, but the source of it, settled there, bore its many hardships – and created strong new nations. By the beginning of the 18th century, North America's true riches had been discovered: fish and fur; timber and tobacco; waterways and good, rich land. And later, too, there would be gold . . .

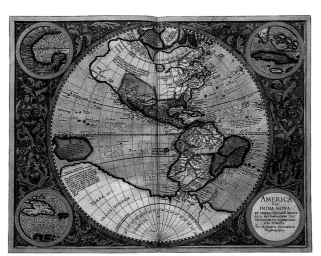

## A LASTING LEGACY

When the new world maps were drawn by the German cartographer Martin Waldseemüller in 1507, he accepted Vespucci's claims and called the new southern continent 'America'. Soon the name was used throughout Europe for all the newly discovered western lands. Vespucci may not have been the first to reach the mainland of America, but his name alone has assured his place in history.

## THE FIVE NATIONS

The five Indian nations which formed the Iroquois
League were the Mohawk, Seneca, Oneida,
Onondaga and Cayuga peoples of the American
Northeast. Iroquois legend tells of how the warring
nations were brought together by a divine messenger,
called the Peacemaker, helped by two tribal leaders,
Tsiskonseseh and Aiontwatha. Immortalized in
Longfellow's epic poem, Aiontwatha became
known as Hiawatha, the Singer of Songs,
who calmed the evil Onondaga Chief
Atotahoh with a Hymn of Peace.
Then Hiawatha combed the
snakes from Atotahoh's hair.
The Peacemakers turned
evil to good by making
the strong, but
vanquished, Atotahoh a
Peace Chief – and the five nations
grew strong.

## CEREMONY AND RITUAL

The Iroquois
sought balance
in all things –
between people
and nature, men
and women, good
and evil. They used
music, dance, songs and
art to create and celebrate
this balance. Masks like this
one were used in False Face
ceremonies to turn away
unkind spirits.

## JOURNEY FROM THE NORTH

The Indian nations told stories.
They built a culture on myth and
legend, handed down in painting
and crafts, dance and
song, and spoken
tales of the
fireside. They all
remembered their
northern ancestors,
and the history of their
beginning became their
mythology. The Tewa of the
American Southwest have a song which begins: '*Yonder in the North
there is singing on the lake. Cloud maidens dance upon the shore.
There we take our being...*' In this contemporary painting, the
artist Felipe Davalos celebrates the first migration of the Tewa.
As they travelled south they divided on each side of a great
river – the Winter People to the east, the Summer People
to the west. Where they joined once again, they built
their great pueblo cities.

## INDIANS OF THE PLAINS

Life on the plains was a life on the move, following
buffalo and the seasons. But there was time for
ceremony and clothing for special occasions. Left, a pair
of beaded, quilted Sioux moccasins; right, a decorated
buckshirt shirt worn by a Blackfoot brave.

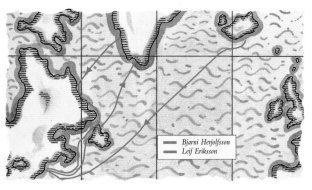

Bjarni Herjolfsson
Leif Eriksson

# THE COMING OF THE NORSEMEN

*f* *rom the fury of the Northmen, O Lord, deliver us!*' For three centuries, the inhabitants of Europe had prayed for protection from the ferocity of marauding Vikings. These tall, fair-skinned warriors would swoop upon their unsuspecting neighbours, carrying off goods, ransom and slaves. But their greatest need was for land. Leaving their own harsh mountainous homelands, the Northmen roamed the seas in their dragon ships. The Swedes went east to Russia while the Danes and Norwegians sailed west, to Britain, Ireland and the islands of the North Atlantic. In AD 815 they began a series of migrations, settling first in Iceland where they built successful new colonies, and on to Greenland. But, tough as they were, the settlers found Greenland a difficult place to live. It was time to set off once again in search of fertile lands. In 1000, Leif Eriksson set out with 35 men to find the lands that Bjarni Herjolfsson had sighted 15 years before. They found Bjarni's land of rocks and ice and called it Helluland (The Land of Rocks). When they stepped onto the barren, rocky shore, Leif said: *'Now we have done better than Bjarni . . . we, at least, have set foot on it!'* The land they stood on was the coast of Labrador – they had discovered North America.

## LEIF ERIKSSON (*c*.970-1020)

Erik the Red's son became North America's first recorded explorer. After he and his party made their first landfall, they sailed on south and found a wooded lowland which he called Markland (Wood Land) – now Nova Scotia – and on to a much more fertile coast. They found fish in abundance and berries. Leif called this soft land, Vinland the Good. No one knows exactly where along the coast of North America Vinland lay, but many scholars now believe that it was on the New England coast at Cape Cod.

## VINLAND

With Leif Eriksson on his journey of discovery was a German called Tyrker, who had looked after Erik's family when he left Iceland. Wandering off on his own, Tyrker found vines and berries – like those he remembered from his childhood in Germany. He told Leif that he had found grapes with which to make wine during the coming winter – thus giving Vinland its name.

## ERIK THE RED

In AD 982, a Viking chief named Erik the Red was banished from Iceland. He went exploring and found another huge island to the west, whose welcoming fjords and fertile summer valleys inspired him to call it 'Greenland', despite the fact that only one-fifth of the land was free of ice.

## NORTH AMERICA
### -A TIME LINE-

~13,000 BC~
*First migration of people from Asia across the land bridge into North America.*

~4,000 BC~
*Eskimos colonize far North.*

~200 BC–AD 1300~
*Anasazi civilization in American Southwest; cliff-dwellings in Mesa Verde.*

~982–985~
*Erik the Red founds the colony in Greenland.*

~985~
*Bjarni Herjolfsson makes first Viking journey to North American coast.*

~1000–1003~
*Following Bjarni's route, Leif Eriksson makes landfall on Cape Cod. Vinland colony established but fails.*

## AN ACCIDENTAL DISCOVERY

One young settler, Bjarni Herjolfsson, set out with his crew from Iceland to Greenland in AD 985. Three days from land the fair winds died and his ship was carried southward by the current. Drifting into a huge bank of fog, they lost their bearings for many days. When the fog lifted, they lay off the coast of a low, wooded land – not Greenland, which was both mountainous and icy. They sailed north again, passing a rocky island which did have a glacier. Bjarni pronounced it 'worthless'. A four-day gale brought them miraculously to their destination – having visited the coast of North America on the way!

## EVIDENCE

A good deal of evidence has been found to prove the presence of the Vikings in North America. Much of it comes from a settlement on the northern tip of Newfoundland, called L'Anse aux Meadows. Its site, on such a storm-lashed coast, suggests that it was a temporary settlement founded by colonists whose ships were swept down the Straits of Belle Isle by the strong Labrador current. Other sites have been found as far north as Ellesmere Island off the Arctic coast of Canada.

## LA ISABELA

Christopher Columbus spent seven long years pleading his cause before King Ferdinand and Queen Isabella of Spain. *'I plough on,'* he said bitterly, *'no matter how the winds might lash me.'* He knew that the Spanish rulers were his last hope of realizing his ambition. At last they agreed, thus giving Spain an unexpected advantage in the coming race for power and riches. In honour of his patron, Columbus named his first, short-lived settlement – on the West Indian island of Hispaniola – *La Isabela*.

## THE WORLD AFTER COLUMBUS

Columbus's voyages began a period of European exploration that lasted for 300 years. Long before it was over, geographers claimed that they could now map the whole world. This map, drawn in 1608, incorporates a century of new information about the Americas. It is confidently titled '*A new Geographical and Hydrographic Map of All the Known Lands of the Globe*'.

## NEW WORLD PLANTS

Unusual New World fruits and vegetables became much more than curiosities to the first explorers and early settlers. In time, many of the staple plants of the Indians – such as maize, potatoes and tobacco – would be introduced into Europe in the form of both plants and seeds. Others, like the Cassava root, agave, prickly pear and pineapple were also introduced with some success. Sweet potatoes were brought back as early as 1493 when Christopher Columbus returned to Spain.

## ASTROLABE

An astrolabe is a mechanical working model of the movement of heavenly bodies. By measuring the exact position of the sun or a bright star, mariners could plot their position at sea. They were first used by ancient Greek and Arab navigators. The Portuguese devised an updated version that was widely used by the mariners of Columbus's time.

# COLUMBUS PAVES THE WAY

*Columbus landing in South America*

**C**hristopher Columbus (1451-1506) did not discover America – that happened 15,000 years before his journey began. He wasn't the first European to reach the New World – that had happened at least 500 years earlier. Nor, on any of his four voyages, did he ever reach the North American mainland itself – that would happen seven years after his death. What, then, was the significance of the cry of *Tierra! Tierra!* (Land! Land!) that rang out from the first of his three small ships in the pre-dawn light of 12 October 1492?

By the middle of the 15th century, the idea that the earth was round – and not flat – was generally accepted by scientists and mathematicians. Sailors were more sceptical. But Columbus believed, not only that the world was round, but also that he could reach the East by sailing west. He was equally certain that God had *'revealed to me that it was feasible to sail ... to the Indies, and placed in me a burning desire to carry out this plan!'* He was right. But how difficult it was. It could only have been accomplished by a man of stubborn self-belief, and a navigator of genius. And the consequence of Columbus's mistaken discovery in 1492? It doubled the size of the known world – and changed the course of history.

## THE NAVIGATOR OF GENOA

Born in the Italian seaport of Genoa, Columbus was the son of a master weaver, but the sea was his passion. He spent nine years learning from the Portuguese, the most accomplished navigators in the world. During those years, his obsession was born. He was bright, enthusiastic, curious and impressive – six feet tall with red hair, and a burning ambition.

## CARAVELS

The three small ships used by Columbus on his voyage to the New World were caravels – known as explorer's ships. Designed by Portuguese shipbuilders, the caravel was small, light, fast and easy to sail. Columbus sailed in three ships: the *Niña* (nickname of the *Santa Clara*), the *Pinta* and the *Santa Maria*, whose fame is assured wherever his great feat of seamanship is mentioned.

# THE TUDOR VENTURERS

### SIR FRANCIS DRAKE
### (1540-1596)

Much more of an adventurer than an explorer, Francis Drake became one of the most feared – and successful – pirates of the 16th century. With the secret encouragement of Queen Elizabeth I, Drake looted the Spanish treasure ships laden with gold from the New World. During several voyages to the West Indies in the 1570s, Drake attacked the Spaniards on the high seas and besieged them in their home ports.

While the Spanish and Portuguese were staking their claims in South America – and likely to control any southern trade routes to the East – other European monarchs looked north. It was important to both the English and the French to find what they believed was the key to unimaginable wealth and power: the shortest trade route to the spicelands of the Orient. King Henry VII of England decided to do a little exploring of his own, and another Italian was on hand to help him. John Cabot made two voyages to the New World, sailing due west from the British Isles. He explored the coasts of Newfoundland and Nova Scotia and touched the North American mainland before returning home. His claim that he had reached the '*land of the Great Khan*' was mistaken, but his claim to lands in the name of an English monarch opened the way for centuries of exploration and colonization of the eastern coast of North America – perhaps the most important discovery of all.

### MARTIN FROBISHER (*c.*1535-1594)

Frobisher was a contemporary of Drake and one of the first of the English navigators to make a true search for the longed-for Northwest Passage. He made three attempts to reach Asia by sailing northwest. He failed but his voyages greatly extended the geographical knowledge of Greenland and the northern coast of Canada. He discovered Frobisher Bay on Baffin Island. Frobisher was lured away from the task of further exploration by the discovery of a golden rock on his first voyage in 1576. He returned twice more to fill his ships with the ore – but, alas, what he had carried back to England was only 'fool's gold'.

## CODFISH AHOY!

*'The sea is swarming with fish, which can be taken not only with the net but in baskets let down with a stone. . .'* This was how one of the sailors on John Cabot's first voyage described their arrival in the rich fishing grounds off the Canadian Coast. Fishing fleets soon followed to create the first major industry in North America. Their logs and records helped mapmakers prepare much more accurate charts for later voyages of discovery.

### JOHN CABOT (1425-*c*.1500)

Italian by birth and a mapmaker and merchant by trade, Giovanni Caboto brought his young family to Bristol in the 1480s, where he became John Cabot, navigator. Inspired by Columbus's voyage in 1492, Cabot set out to search for a northerly route to Asia. Backed by the English king – who granted Cabot and his sons *'full and free authority leave and power. . . to seek out, discover and find whatsoever isles, countries, regions or provinces of the heathen and infidels...'* in exchange for one-fifth of all profits. He was financed by the merchants of England's busiest seaport and sailed in the *Matthew* from Bristol in 1497.

### NEW ALBION

On the orders of his queen, Drake set out in 1577 on his greatest adventure – to sail through the Straits of Magellan and surprise the Spaniards. His task successfully completed, he sailed up the California coast as far as Canada, hoping to find a shorter route back to England. Finding none, Drake returned to California for repairs. Laying a somewhat casual claim to the land around the Spanish settlement of San Francisco, he renamed it New Albion. But Drake was no colonist and 'New Albion' lasted hardly longer than his fleeting visit to North America.

## NORTH AMERICA
### -A TIME LINE-

~1451~
*Christopher Columbus born in Genoa.*

~1492~
*Columbus's historic voyage across the Atlantic Ocean. Lands in the Bahamas convinced he has reached the Indies.*

~1497~
*John Cabot explores the east coast of Canada.*

~1501~
*Amerigo Vespucci names the western continent* Mundus Novus *(the New World); his name goes onto map of 1507.*

~1513~
*Juan Ponce de Léon becomes first European to reach North American mainland since Vikings; discovers* La Florida.

~1524~
*Giovanni da Verrazano explores northeast coast; discovers New York Bay and Narragansett Bay.*

### NAVIGATIONAL INSTRUMENTS

Tudor explorers were helped on their voyage by several navigational aids such as compasses, solar and lunar dials and astrolabes. This unusual brass compendium of astronomical instruments was made by Humphrey Cole in 1569.

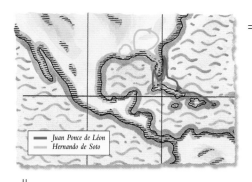

Juan Ponce de Léon
Hernando de Soto

# SPAIN IN NORTH AMERICA: *LA FLORIDA*

The discoveries made by Christopher Columbus gave Spain an important advantage in the exploration of the 'Indies' – especially over her old rivals Portugal. By the early 1500s many more expeditions were underway to exploit the possibilities of the New World. Some were made by people who had sailed with Columbus, such as Juan Ponce de Léon who colonized and governed Puerto Rico before setting out in 1513 to explore the islands to the north, searching for gold. Instead he made a momentous discovery and became the first European to stand on the mainland of North America since the Norsemen left 500 years before. But this southern land was very different – lush, green and tropical. He called it *La Florida*. However, in those early days, the main thrust of Spanish exploration was in Central and South America. Inspired by legends of vast treasure in the lands to the west, the Spanish were spectacularly successful. In a little more than a decade (1521-1533) they had conquered and plundered the great civilizations of Mexico and Peru. Fuelled by Indian legends of *El Dorado*, their ambitions grew with each success. It was time to explore *La Florida*.

### HERNANDO DE SOTO

The man who led the Florida expedition was Hernando de Soto (*c*.1500-1542) who was one of the richest men in Spain. But he also wanted a seat of power in the New World, and the King of Spain offered him *La Florida* – to be conquered, held and governed at his own expense. De Soto accepted, raised an army which was the '*youngest, best equipped and most professional ever to sail from Spain*', and landed at Tampa Bay in 1539.

## THE SPANISH EMPIRE

By 1600, the Spanish Empire of *La Florida* was enormous – stretching from the Atlantic to the Pacific Ocean and from the Gulf of Mexico to Chesapeake Bay. Constantly under attack over the next 200 years, it became part of the United States in 1821.

## THE MIGHTY MISSISSIPPI

For three years De Soto's remarkable army wandered further into the northern continent than any Europeans before them – fighting their way through swamps and forests, and meeting both welcome and ambush from the native tribes along the way. And always there were tales of the treasures that lay just ahead. At long last, bedraggled and battle-scarred, De Soto and his followers came upon something more important than treasure. On Sunday, 8 May 1541, they stepped out onto the banks of the greatest river that any Spaniard had ever seen. They called it the Rio Grande, but it was already known by its Algonquin name, the Mississippi.

## THE NATIVES OF FLORIDA

*'The people are thus naked, handsome, brown and well formed in body ...'*
John White was one of the first artists to record the New World in the 16th century. He travelled widely and was interested in everything – the plants, animals, and landscape, as well as the life and customs of the native peoples. His drawings provided an accurate study of the people whom the first visitors met when they landed in the New World.

## THE FOUNTAIN OF YOUTH

Like so many of his intrepid countrymen, Juan Ponce de Léon (1460-1521) set out on his voyage northward dreaming of wealth and glory. The Spanish had many legends but there was one which took his fancy – that somewhere to the north was a magical spring whose pure waters would ensure eternal youth. He may well have found sparkling waters of healthy mineral springs, but what is certain is that he found the land of 'Florida' – part of what is now the United States of America.

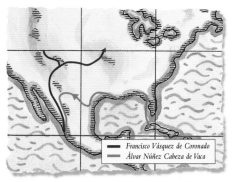

Francisco Vásquez de Coronado
Álvar Núñez Cabeza de Vaca

# THE GOLDEN PROMISE

Someone who listened with interest to the tales of golden treasure to be found beyond the mountains of Mexico was Francisco Vásquez de Coronado (*c.*1510-1554). Sent by the Viceroy of Mexico, he set out in 1540 to push north in search of the fabled 'seven cities of Cíbola' – a legend of riches that all Spain knew, now given new life by the successful plundering of Mexico and Peru. There must be cities of equal wonder in the unknown lands to the north, and he would find them! For two years his party was driven onward, through the white heat of the southern desert and up into the Great Plains of present-day Oklahoma and Kansas, but their search was in vain. However, they did find things that no European had ever seen: great open lands of tall grass, vast herds of buffalo and the mysterious pueblo cities of the Zuni. They even stumbled upon a still greater wonder – the Grand Canyon. But they found no gold. Coronado saw his expedition as a failure, later saying, '*It was God's pleasure that these discoveries should remain for other peoples.*' His words might stand as a epitaph for the whole of the Spanish adventure in North America.

### STRANDED

Álvar Núñez Cabeza de Vaca (*c.*1490-1560) was a member of an ill-fated expedition to explore the coast of Florida. Shipwrecked in 1528 on the Texas coast, de Vaca and three companions were enslaved by the local tribes for the next five years before escaping. Then they began to walk. They walked across the Mexican Peninsula, reaching the Gulf of California in 1536. They became, by accident, the first Europeans to cross the North American continent from the Atlantic to the Pacific.

## CORONADO'S MARCH

Coronado's party was impressive. Joining him on the arduous journey from Mexico were 336 Spaniards and 1,000 native bearers, guides and interpreters.

## CORONADO'S LEGACY

When the first settlers made their way to Texas and New Mexico in the early 1800s, they were astonished to find huge herds of small, tough horses roaming wild on the plains. These were the 'mustangs', descendants of the 1,500 Spanish horses that carried Coronado and his party on their journey through the Southwest. Coronado's horses were of Arab blood - strong and intelligent. By training mustangs, the Indian braves became the heirs to the great Spanish tradition of horsemanship – and formidable warriors.

## NORTH AMERICA
### -A Time Line-

*~1535~*
*Jacques Cartier discovers the St. Lawrence River; establishes Montreal for France.*

*~1539–1542~*
*Hernando de Soto explores American Southeast; discovers the Mississippi in 1541, dies there in 1542.*

*~1540~*
*Coronado discovers the Grand Canyon.*

*~1576~*
*Martin Frobisher searches for Northwest Passage; discovers Frobisher Bay on Baffin Island.*

*Francis Drake claims Spanish settlement at San Francisco as 'New Albion'.*

*~1586–1587~*
*First English colonies on Roanoke Island in Virginia, none survive. Virginia Dare born 1587.*

## GRAND CANYON

Coronado's native guides shared their legends of great cities, huge grasslands and natural wonders – but the Spaniards valued only gold. Their searches took them through uncharted areas of the American Southwest – all claimed for the King of Spain. It was a landscape of stark and unimaginable beauty. At its heart lay the Grand Canyon, created over millions of years by the winding Colorado River cutting its way through the soft, vari-coloured rocks. It is now 446 kilometres long, and up to 1.5 kilometres deep. Even the treasure-seeking Spaniards must have gasped in awe at such a sight.

# THE FRENCH IN CANADA

**GIOVANNI DA VERRAZANO**
*(c.1485-1528)*

Eleven years before Cartier's expedition, the Italian Giovanni da Verrazano sailed to the New World on behalf of the French king, Francis I. He explored the eastern coast of the new continent, trying to find a passage leading westward. He explored New York Bay and Narragansett Bay – and travelled as far south as Carolina – but the long coastline remained unbroken.

The French, like the English, wanted to find a shorter, northern route to the riches of the East. In 1535, the French explorer Jacques Cartier (1491-1557) ventured further north. Beyond Newfoundland, he came upon an undiscovered waterway. It was a huge river, later called the St Lawrence. In small boats, Cartier and his men sailed more than 1,600 kilometres deep into the heart of the continent. From a vantage point high above the river rapids, Cartier looked out over a vast land of dense forests and broad inland seas. He named the spot Mount Royal (Montreal). Cartier's four expeditions allowed France to claim large areas of land, which became known as New France – the heart of French presence in North America. Cartier, like so many others, was looking for a way *around* the new continent and not at the possibilities to be found within it. But those who followed began to see where true wealth lay – in the natural resources of the New World. They created a great trading empire based, not on plunder, but on trade alliance with the Indians, who dealt in another precious commodity – fur.

## DOWN THE MISSISSIPPI

The motivation for the early exploration of the Mississippi River was mainly for personal gain. But there were others with a wider vision. Réne-Robert Cavelier de la Salle (1643-1687) was obsessed with the idea of creating a chain of linked trading posts along the banks of the Mississippi. He travelled its full length from Quebec to the Gulf of Mexico – and back again. In 1682 he claimed the whole of the Mississippi Valley for France, naming it for his king. The great Louisiana territory was born.

## THE INLAND SEAS

In 1608, Samuel de Champlain (c.1567-1635) founded the first permanent colony in New France at Quebec, as a trading outpost. Champlain learned from Indian guides of several large bodies of water which lay to the south and west. He first saw the 200-kilometres-long Lake Champlain in 1609. Following the St Lawrence west in 1615, Champlain entered the system of huge lakes now known as the Great Lakes. Later French explorers threaded their way deep into the Canadian wilderness by following the intricate, interlocking system of waterways – along which trade would flow for centuries to come.

# THE ENGLISH COLONIES

### THE PEACEABLE KINGDOM

Painted by the Quaker artist Edward Hicks, *The Peaceable Kingdom* reflects his view of the early colonies. The English had a difficult time 'taking root' in the New World, but the virtues of fortitude, good sense, honesty and religious conviction helped them succeed. These qualities along with their language and culture – were the priceless legacy of those first English settlers.

It was some time after Cabot's voyage of discovery for Henry VII that the English began to show serious interest in the New World. Sir Walter Raleigh, flamboyant favourite of Queen Elizabeth I, sponsored three attempts to establish a permanent English settlement. The first two attempts to Roanoke Island in Virginia were unsuccessful, as the colonists found poor land and seas too shallow for good fishing. In 1587, a third expedition sailed for Chesapeake Bay further north, led by the artist John White and his family. The ship's captain refused to sail north and once again put the 117 colonists down at the ill-fated Roanoke site. Twenty-seven days later, John White's daughter Eleanor gave birth to the first English child born in America – named Virginia Dare. White went back to England for supplies but, when he returned, the colony had vanished. White and his men found the word CROATOAN carved on a tree – it was the name of a friendly Indian tribe. No trace of the Lost Colony was ever found, and Roanoke was abandoned. In 1607, English colonists reached Chesapeake Bay at last and established, in this more temperate land, the first permanent English colony at Jamestown, named in honour of the new king.

### THE TOBACCO ECONOMY

The Virginia colony had among its members people with the skills to create a new community. In John Smith (1580-1631) they found a leader with common sense. He insisted that everyone worked and established a 'tobacco economy' – with a tithe of each crop used to support projects for the whole community. It was the first local tax levied in the colonies and helped Jamestown to be self-sufficient.

### PLIMOTH PLANTATION

The first English colony in what became New England – the heart of English North America – was founded on an accidental landing on a low wooded spit of land just as winter was drawing in. What they had found was a good land – as Leif Eriksson had found it 600 years before – and having nowhere else to go, they stayed, survived, and prospered.

## VIRGINIA

This map, or 'platt' of the 'South Part of Virginia' was painted on vellum by Nicholas Comberford in 1657. It shows in some detail the area of the coast surrounding Roanoke Island – the site of the first English colony in North America – as well as Albemarle Sound, Pimlico Sound and the long, thin islands of Cape Hatteras. In 1673, Charles II made this area a part of the new colony of Carolina. It is now part of the distinctive coastline of North Carolina.

## ARTIST OF THE NEW WORLD

The English artist John White was a member of the first of Raleigh's expeditions to Virginia. He was an enthusiastic colonist and was expected to use his skills to attract other settlers to the new colony. His numerous drawings and delicate watercolour paintings are naturalistic and well-observed. White chose to concentrate on the more domestic aspects of Indian life and customs, as in this depiction of the Village of Secoton, painted in 1587, with its well-ordered fields and neat huts. The inhabitants danced in a formal ceremony around posts 'carved on the topps lyke mens faces.'

## THE MAYFLOWER PILGRIMS

The *Mayflower* sailed from Plymouth, England on 15 August 1620. After its companion ship *Speedwell* began to leak, the *Mayflower* continued on alone across the Atlantic. It carried 102 passengers, many religious reformers. They were heading towards Chesapeake Bay and the colony at Jamestown, but made landfall instead at Provincetown on Cape Cod on 21 November 1620. Exploring the coast, they chose a site for a new colony, which they called Plimoth.

# HENRY HUDSON: EXPLORATION & ENTERPRISE

By the beginning of the 1600s, the exploration of North America had become an increasingly commercial affair. In place of the haphazard adventures undertaken by mercenary dreamers backed by rulers looking to enhance their power, came well-planned expeditions financed by groups of speculators and sober trading companies. What had been a chaotic every-man-for-himself scramble for personal gain and glory, became a business opportunity. Yet the one thing that *all* the new backers wanted to find was the Northwest Passage. Between 1607 and 1611 the explorer and sea-captain Henry Hudson made four voyages to North America, which took him to within 1,110 kilometres of the North Pole – further north than any other European had ventured. His attempts to find a navigable westward passage failed, but he discovered the true reason why the route to the East might never be found – ice! Hudson's journeys were of crucial importance for the future of the two countries – Holland and England. Hudson was hired by trading companies in both countries: his discovery of the Hudson River gave the Dutch their first real foothold in North America; his final voyage enabled England to claim both the Hudson Strait and the vast inland sea known as Hudson Bay.

## LANDFALL!

Henry Hudson undertook his third voyage for the Dutch East India Company and landed at the mouth of the Hudson River in 1609. Disappointed by his failure to find a northern route which would link them with their interests in the East, the Dutch abandoned further exploration. They did, however, claim the land he explored on his run southward along the Atlantic coast – including the Hudson River valley and the site of what would become New Amsterdam (later New York).

J212, 411

## FAMILIAR AND EXOTIC ANIMALS

Many of the animals which European explorers found in the North American woodlands would have been familiar – wolves, bears, foxes and the beavers so greatly prized for their luxuriant fur.

## TRADING POSTS

Built on trade alliances with Indian fur trappers, the Hudson's Bay Company built a network of trading posts, known as Houses or Forts. The terms of trade were set in brass tokens linked to the value of a beaver skin. In some areas, goods could be paid for with the Company's own pound notes!

## ALEXANDER MACKENZIE (1764-1820)

The huge area of western Canada was opened to traders and settlers as a result of expeditions made by the Scottish explorer, Alexander Mackenzie. Beginning at Lake Athabasca in the centre of the Canadian wilderness, Mackenzie travelled by water to Great Slave Lake and out onto the broad river which bears his name. Convinced that the westward-flowing river would carry him to the Pacific Ocean, Mackenzie was dismayed when it began to curve northward. He called it the 'River of Disappointment'. Nevertheless, he travelled the whole of its length, finally sighting the Arctic Ocean in 1789, having travelled 1,700 kilometres. Mackenzie eventually crossed the continent from east to west in 1793.

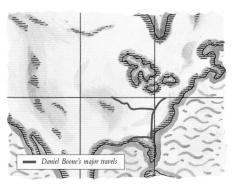

Daniel Boone's major travels

# DANIEL BOONE & THE WILDERNESS ROAD

Once the English colonies on the eastern seaboard began to thrive, more and more settlers arrived to make new lives in North America. For more than a century they poured into the lands governed by the English Crown – lands that lay between the Atlantic Ocean and the great spine of the Appalachian Mountains which ran from New England to the Georgia forests. What lay beyond was a matter for speculation: dense, uncharted woodlands, wild beasts, and Indian tribes of uncertain temper? Perhaps even the Pacific Ocean? The pressure for more and more land for settlers was growing and, in spite of English disapproval, people began to think about 'going west'. It was Daniel Boone (1734-1820) who showed them the way. He was born in Pennsylvania into a family about whom it was said: '*They had an itching foot. Something called. Something beyond the mountains always whispered.*' In 1775, after years of wandering through wilderness no white man had ever entered, Boone led a party of 30 woodsmen across the mountains. They cleared and connected a complex network of Indian trails and animal pathways to cut the first road leading from the Virginia colonies across the mountains to the Tennessee River Valley and on to Kentucky. Almost 500 kilometres long, it became known as the Wilderness Road. It was the gateway west.

## AN EARTHLY PARADISE

Once Boone saw the wild wooded hills of Kentucky, he was determined to bring his family there to live in this land he called a '*second paradise*'. By 1800, more than 200,000 pioneers had followed Daniel Boone down the Wilderness Road.

## HUNTIN', TRAPPIN' AND WANDERIN'

Daniel Boone spent many years of his life following these three favourite pastimes. To enjoy them he needed very few things: a good flintlock rifle, a hunting knife and a strong hunting bag made of macramé and leather in which to carry game. Boone 'wandered' a good deal – as far south as Florida and westward into the Missouri Valley. In 1769, Boone and a few hunting companions crossed the Appalachian Mountains at Cumberland Gap (discovered in 1750 by Dr Thomas Walker) and down into Kentucky. It was a hunting trip that became a two-year exploration of a huge area of the wilderness that lay beyond the mountains – where the Old West began.

## THE FRONTIERSMAN

Daniel Boone's son Nathan described his father as being '*five feet eight inches high, with broad shoulders and chest ...(weighing) about one hundred and seventy-five pounds...eyes blue and skin fair.*' Certainly a well-grown and well-favoured man for his time, but so great was his reputation, that he was often described as being huge in stature. In spite of its obvious dangers, his tough frontier life was a healthy one and he lived to the remarkable age of 85. His sharp sense of humour must have helped, too! When the itinerant painter Chester Harding came to paint his portrait in the last year of Boone's life, he asked the famous woodsman if he had ever got lost in the forests: '*No*', answered Boone, '*I can't say that I was ever lost, but I was* bewildered *once for three days.*'

## NORTH AMERICA
### -A Time Line-

*~1600~*
*Spanish empire of La Florida largest in North America.*

*~1607~*
*First English colony at Jamestown on Chesapeake Bay; John Smith leader, colony survives.*

*~1608–1615~*
*Samuel de Champlain founds Quebec Colony; discovers Lake Champlain and Great Lakes.*

*French establish fur trading empire in Canada.*

*~1609–1611~*
*Henry Hudson searches for Northwest Passage; discovers Hudson River, Hudson Strait and Hudson Bay.*

*~1620~*
Mayflower *pilgrims land at Provincetown on 21 November; establish Plimoth Plantation.*

*~1670~*
*Hudson's Bay Company created by Royal Charter.*

*~1679–1682~*
*De la Salle explores Mississippi valley; claims for France, becomes Louisiana Territory.*

*~1775~*
*Daniel Boone creates the Wilderness Road.*

*~1776~*
*Declaration of Independence – Thirteen Colonies win their independence from Britain.*

*~1793~*
*Alexander Mackenzie follows the Mackenzie River to the Arctic Ocean.*

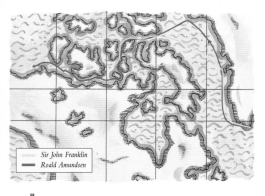

Sir John Franklin
Roald Amundsen

# THE SEARCH FOR THE NORTHWEST PASSAGE

*T*he Holy Grail of North American exploration for almost 500 years, the Northwest Passage defeated generations of geographers, navigators and 'arctic experts' from all over Northern Europe. But no nation tried so hard and risked so much as the English in their dogged quest. For 300 years after Frobisher's voyages in the 1570s, English mariners continued to push their way north, through the icy seas and along the inhospitable coast of North America. Ever seeking that perfect route across the top of the world which would give them access to the East, they explored every part of the Canadian Arctic. As the French and the English began to explore and colonize the lands they had claimed, the huge continent became less of a hindrance and more of an opportunity. Interest in finding the Northwest Passage appeared to dwindle – until the early 1800s. The most famous and tragic of these adventures was the third expedition made by Sir John Franklin in 1845. After two successful ventures, he returned to the Arctic determined to find, at long last, a way through the icebound straits from east to west. In fact, the expedition achieved its objective, but their success remained unknown for a decade. There was no one left alive to tell the tale.

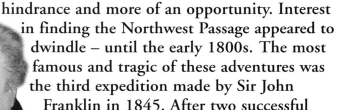

### THE REWARD

In 1817 the British parliament offered a reward of £5,000 to the first ship to cross longitude 110°W, north of the polar circle. The challenge was taken up by John Ross the following year, but his two ships failed to defeat the pack-ice. Ross's second-in-command, Edward Parry, made another attempt. This time, as he set off by sea, he sent John Franklin (1786-1847) overland from Hudson Bay to the coast. Parry set out in May 1819, crossed the 110° line and won the reward. Franklin continued on and surveyed the arctic coast for three full years – a journey of some 8,800 kilometres. Their discoveries made accurate mapping of the northern coast of Canada possible.

In 1845, Sir John Franklin set out on his most ambitious voyage. With 129 companions, he sailed in *Erebus* and *Terror* to find the Northwest Passage. Nothing was heard from the expedition and so, with hope fading for the safe return of her husband, Lady Franklin appealed to the British Admiralty for help. With their backing, and that of the President of the United States, a great search was launched in 1847. It lasted more than 10 years and involved 40 ships. Finally, the crew of the *Fox* found Franklin's last message in a cairn of rocks on King William Island which told of their cruel fate.

## THE LAST DAYS

Abandoning the icebound ships, the men had walked for 250 kilometres eastward towards the open sea. *Erebus* and *Terror* were never found. Their last days were commemorated in this painting by W Thomas Smith, dramatically titled *They Forged the Last Link With Their Lives*.

### SUCCESS!

The Norwegian explorer Roald Amundsen (1872-1928) spent two years (1903-1905) living among the Eskimos of King William Island, making notes and taking measurements. When he was ready, Amundsen and a party of six set out on 13 August 1905 in an old fishing boat, the *Gjoa*. They sailed westward through the straits until they came to open sea. The Northwest Passage had been conquered by boat – but by then it was almost too late. Within 10 years the Panama Canal was built. It would carry ships laden with goods and passengers quickly from one great ocean to the other, fanned by tropical breezes rather than icy Arctic winds.

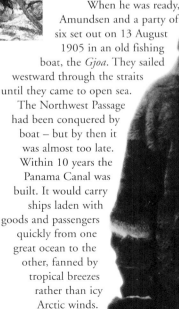

## BANNER OF HOPE

Sir John Franklin was fortunate in having a determined and devoted wife who refused to give up the search for her missing husband. As well as sending ships to the rescue, Lady Franklin embroidered this flag, carried by the HMS *John Barrow* as it journeyed north. It is a symbol of her unceasing efforts to learn of the fate of the expedition.

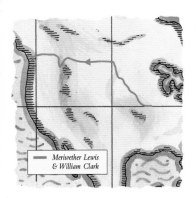

Meriwether Lewis
& William Clark

# LEWIS AND CLARK: ACROSS THE CONTINENT

*'Your mission is to explore the Missouri River, and such principal stream of it, as by its course...may offer the most direct and practicable water communication across this continent, for the purposes of commerce.'*

Jefferson, Pr. U. S. of America, 20 June 1803

With this formal commission, Thomas Jefferson, third president of the United States, set in motion the first real phase of exploration under the government of the new republic. A year later, the Corps of Discovery set out on its daunting but successful three-year mission – to explore and survey the land west of the Mississippi. The vast Louisiana Territory had changed hands several times, with all the land east of the Mississippi ceded to the new United States after the War of Independence. By 1801, the remainder had fallen into the hands of Napoleon. Jefferson distrusted the French emperor and concluded what must rank as one of the shrewdest property deals in history – in 1803 he made the Louisiana Purchase for just $16,000,000, more than doubling the size of the United States. Now his, he wanted an expedition to explore it. He entrusted the task to his young Secretary, Captain Meriwether Lewis. With him went Lieutenant William Clark. It was the mission of a lifetime.

### THE NATURALIST AND THE GEOGRAPHER

Throughout their 12,400-kilometre journey, both expedition leaders took detailed notes of their surroundings. Meriwether Lewis (1774-1809) was the naturalist, noting the richness and diversity of the plant and animal life. William Clark (1770-1838) was a brilliant draftsman, cartographer and expert geographer who kept detailed notes of all physical features of the journey in his carefully prepared journals.

## THE CORPS OF DISCOVERY

Led by army officers Lewis (left) and Clark (right), the 45 members of the Corps of Discovery included men with experience in many other trades useful on the long journey ahead. There were carpenters, smiths, hunters, hide-curers and tailors, as well as experts in the universal signing language of the Plains Indians. They left nothing to chance – building camps in which to winter and designing a special flat-bottomed keelboat, which could be rowed, sailed or poled.

## ACROSS THE ROCKIES

Setting out from the St Louis camp in May 1804, the expedition followed the broad Missouri River north into the lands of the Dakotas. There they wintered, to harden themselves in preparation for the push across the Rockies, and to forge friendly alliances with Indian tribes. Lewis and Clark knew that their success and safety could depend upon the friendship of Indian braves. And so it proved – again and again 'Long Knife' (Lewis) and 'Red Hair' (Clark) had reason to be grateful for their help. In the summer of 1805 they carried their boats over the Rocky Mountains and followed the Columbia River to the sea. That November they came to the Pacific Ocean.

## SACAJAWEA

Passing through Indian country, the expedition relied heavily in its French guides and interpreters, George Drouillard and Toussaint Charbonneau. With him came Charbonneau's young Indian wife and her baby son as a sign that this was not a war party. Sacajawea was a Shoshone who had been captured by raiders as a girl. In the summer of 1805, as they moved closer to the Rockies – Shoshone country – the land became more and more familiar to her. The expedition needed to purchase Shoshone horses to take them across the mountains. When at last they met with a party of warriors, Sacajawea recognized her own people. She came forward to interpret before any threat could be made. A tense moment turned into one of joy, their chief was her own elder brother – Sacajawea had come home.

## THE PATHFINDER

John Charles Frémont was a captain in the U S Army Topographical Engineering Corps, who explored and surveyed much of the huge area west of the Rockies. He charted the Oregon Trail – the longest, and toughest, of the great overland routes used by pioneers in the great westward expansion of the United States in the mid-19th century. In 1842, Frémont made the first full survey of the Wind River chain of the Rocky Mountains, making the first ascent of Frémont Peak. He later mapped both Nevada and California. His surveys were so important in the mapping of the American West, that Frémont became known as 'The Pathfinder'.

## THE VANISHING AMERICANS

*'I'm all Injun but my hide'* wrote Charles Marion Russell (1864-1926), the American painter who more than any other celebrated the Indians of the Plains as their way of life changed with the settlement of the West. At 15 the young Russell left his home in St Louis to share the lives of both cowboys and Indians for the next 30 years. His paintings have vitality, accuracy and an unsentimental sympathy. He worked from an insider's understanding and created a body of work which paid homage to all the people who lived closest to the land. A note on one of Russell's Indian studies read: *'This is the only real American. He fought and died for his country – today he has no vote, no country, and is not a citizen, but history will never forget him.'*

# Westward Movement

The success of Lewis and Clark's expedition to cross the continent from St Louis, Missouri to the Pacific coast had far-reaching consequences. More surveying expeditions were mounted and by 1840 the world began to realize just how vast the new continent was – stretching for more than 4,500 kilometres from the Atlantic to the Pacific, and 2,500 kilometres from the Great Lakes to the Gulf of Mexico. There was land enough for everyone! Settlers once again set out from the crowded eastern seaboard to take up the challenge of a new life in the West. The Conestoga Wagons began to roll and the pioneers were on the move. Their lives would become the stuff of legend. Their fortitude in the face of enormous hardship and danger became one strong strand in the story of 'how the West was won'. The 'winning' of the West by white settlers – farmers, sheepherders and cattlemen – meant the division of land, ownership of grazing and, worst of all, fences. It meant the end of a centuries-old way of life for the Indians.

**KIT CARSON (1809-1868)**

During his travels to the Rockies, Frémont met Kit Carson who became his official guide for the later expeditions. One of the West's great characters, Carson was small, tough and indefatigable. He became a famous Long Hunter, Indian fighter and explorer of the lesser-known areas of the uncharted West. He fought in the Civil War – in full general's uniform, but preferred his comfortable fringed buckskins. It is said that, at his end, Kit ate a prime steak, drank a bowl of coffee, puffed on a final pipe – and died.

# MANIFEST DESTINY

**ZEBULON PIKE**
**(1779-1813)**

Pike mapped the territory from Missouri southwest to the Rockies, and gave his name to the highest peak in 1806.

The great westward movement carried the settlers across the country to California and Oregon – following the Santa Fe and Oregon Trails west. They were joined by thousands of new immigrants from northern Europe – Scandinavian, German, Dutch and Irish settlers joined the great wave of people moving west. In 1870 the population of the territory west of the Mississippi River was 7,000,000; within 20 years it had risen to more than 17,000,000. Always looking for a better life, these new settlers were constantly ready to move on, to take a chance on the unknown. No longer rooted to the place they were born, they identified themselves with the whole country – becoming truly 'Americans'. Oregon was ceded to the United States by Britain in 1846 and the final part of the old Spanish territories won from Mexico in 1848. In 1890, the United States Bureau of Census reported officially that there were 'no frontiers left' – and thus America had fulfilled its Manifest Destiny to control the whole of its continental territory from 'sea to shining sea'. The great age of North American exploration was over.

## THE CONFLICT BEGINS

During the Expansion Era, eastern tribes were forced to move to lands beyond the Mississippi. The hunting grounds of the Great Plains became grazing lands for cattle. The Indian nations suffered great hardship and loss as they left their tribal homelands and moved onward towards an uncertain future. While the pioneers were spurred on by the promise of new lands to gain, the Indians journeyed because of the loss of theirs. It was a recipe for conflict.

### LITTLE WOLF (1820-1904)

A Cheyenne Chief, Little Wolf became one of the leaders of the Indian resistance to white settlement of the West. He spent much of his long life at war, escaping death many times.

### THE OREGON TRAIL

Urged on by the claims of land promoters to come and settle in 'the loveliest country on Earth', thousands of settlers set off from Independence Missouri to travel the 3,000-kilometre Oregon Trail to the Pacific. Huge trains of wagons with horses, livestock and families assembled for the journey – most of which would be accomplished on foot by these hardy and determined people. In 1843 the first big migration began when 900 settlers, with all their worldly belongings, left Missouri. Thousands more followed every year. The beauty of the landscape they travelled through was undeniable – but its grandeur could not mask the danger and hardships, and many people never reached their journey's end.

### KANSAS LAND OFFICE

In May 1862 the US Congress passed the Homestead Act. Under the Act settlers could claim free title to 65 hectares of public land in the western states. In return, they had to stay and cultivate the land for five years. This gave a final boost to the 'land rush', as 500,000 families accepted the government's offer before 1900.

### HEADING FOR A NEW HOME

The covered wagon – its trademark white canvas cover stretched tightly over wooden hoops – became a potent symbol of the westward movement. Stoutly built, these wide-bodied vehicles were both transport and home for many long months. Pioneering families carried all their possessions with them on the journey to Oregon or California. Tight enough to float and tough enough for the harsh terrain, the Conestoga Wagon and its hard-pulling oxen carried many thousands of settlers to a new life in the West.

# DID YOU KNOW?

The early explorers were faced with many strange new places when they first encountered the North American continent. During the centuries these places inspired different names – both descriptive and fanciful – in a number of languages.

**The Atlantic Ocean** was distrusted by mariners throughout history for its fearsome winds and sudden storms. It was known to the Arabs as the 'Sea of Darkness'. The 12th-century Arab geographer Al-Idrissi said of it: '*No one knows what is in that sea, because of many obstacles to navigation – profound darkness, frequent storms, unimaginable monsters…and violent winds.*'

**Labrador** was explored by Jacques Cartier, who found it so bleak he called it 'the land God gave to Cain'.

**Newfoundland** became known as 'Bacalaos' or Codfish-land because of the rich fishing grounds off the Canadian coast.

**The Mississippi River** flowed through the lands of many tribes – Fox, Kickapoo, Iowa, Winnebago, Miami, Oto, Chickasaw and many more. Their names have been borrowed to name the states, cities, towns and rivers of what would become the United States. Each tribe had a different name for the great waterway which runs like a spine through the middle of the continent, but it was the Algonquin name

'*Mississippi*' that stuck. It means 'Big Water' or 'Father of Waters'.

**Virginia and Louisiana** were named after royal patrons. It became the custom for explorers to name newly claimed lands in the new continent after their royal patrons – in the hope of continued favour. The earliest English colonies were established in Virginia, flatteringly named for Queen Elizabeth I, the Virgin Queen. De la Salle claimed the whole of the vast Mississippi valley in the name of Louis XIV of France.

**El Dorado** or 'The Golden One' was a legendary chieftain covered with gold dust, who washed in a sacred lake every evening. This legend lured the Spanish Conquistadores on an endless quest for gold in the New World. In time, El Dorado came to mean both a city of gold, and, as now, simply a dream of riches forever out of reach.

**The Grand Canyon** was named in 1869 by a one-armed geologist, John Wesley Powell. He made the first journey by boat through the great canyons, travelling its full 1,600-kilometre length. Surviving turbulent rapids, deadly whirlpools, capsizing and near starvation, his party fought its way through the huge canyons '*…which unite to form one grand canyon, the most sublime spectacle on Earth.*' It took 98 days.

## ACKNOWLEDGEMENTS

*For Poppaea, a legacy*

J212, 411
£6.00

The publishers wo... ...ish, Jan Alvey and Elizabeth Wiggans for their assistance and David Hobbs for his map of the world.

...ht © 2003 ticktock Entertainment Ltd.

First published i... ...Orchard Business Centre, North Farm Road, Tunbridge Wells, Kent TN2 3XF.

All rights reserve... ...trieval system, or transmitted in any form or by any means electronic, ...en permission of the copyright owner.

A C... ...9 (pbk), ISBN 1 86007 227 5 (pbk)

**snapping-turtle guide**